The Littlest Loon

Text by Robert Kutter

Illustrations by Debra Johnson

Minnesota's state bird, the common loon, is fascinating to observe. Loons arrive at a lake just after ice-out in the spring, establish territory, raise offspring, and migrate south in the fall. Throughout the summer, their calling, feeding, diving and gathering behaviors are fun to observe.

This is the true story of one tiny loon that overcame many obstacles at the beginning of life and thrived.

Text by Robert Kutter, Illustrations by Debra Johnson

Printed in the United States of America by   Sunray Printing Solutions, Inc.
25123 22nd Avenue
Saint Cloud, Minnesota 56301

ISBN-13:   978-0-615-87717-4

Dedicated to grandchildren

Emma and Leighton Kutter

The littlest loon hatched late in June

nearly a month after its cousins.

For several days, the parent loons fed,
protected and nurtured the chick.

Then amid the wavy turmoil of water skiers, jet-ski riders
and pontoon boaters on the Fourth of July,

the littlest loon bobbed alone in the water.

People on the shore shouted, "It's the baby loon! It's the baby loon!" No parent loon was in sight.

Seeing the baby chick in danger,
a man and woman on shore
used field glasses to search
for the parent loons.

Finally spotting an adult loon a half mile away,
the man and woman got in their fishing boat,

sped to the struggling baby loon and
scooped it up with a fishing net.

With the littlest loon cradled in the woman's hand,
the man drove the boat to where the adult loon
had been spotted.

Near the adult loon,
the man stopped the boat,

and the woman gently released
the peeping little loon in the water.

Quicker than lightning, the big loon was at the side of the baby.
Then in a second the other parent was there too.

One day the man and woman spotted
the littlest loon riding on the back of a parent.

As weeks went by, the baby loon
grew bigger and stronger.

August passed into September, and
the littlest loon continued to grow.

The parents migrated south and left
the littlest loon alone to fend for itself.

October came and went, and
the littlest loon had grown big and strong.

Finally, on the 21st of November, the littlest loon flew
from the lake just a week before ice-over.

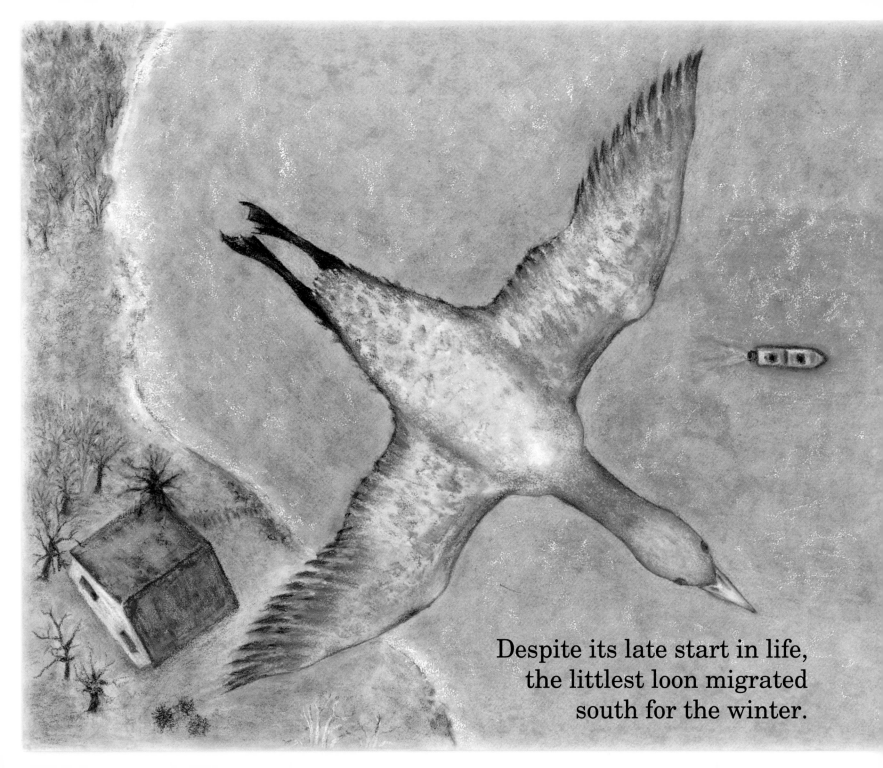

Despite its late start in life,
the littlest loon migrated
south for the winter.